Feeling Blue

Akikya Henderson

Table of Contents

Deeply Disturbed.

You feel like a burden, so you carry a lot of pain within. To you, the pain is too much to bear. It seems unfair for you to be placed with this burden, and you drive yourself crazy trying to understand why your body was chosen as a vessel of suffering. You never see how others suffer on your behalf, how they ache for you. The biggest pain of all is the pain you leave behind. That pain is bigger than the pain you've carried within yourself.

Tired.

Another day, another person I have to ghost.

I hate the fact that it's the ones that I loved the most.

But I love the feel of release when I just let it go.

I'm not perfect; I've made mistakes, just so you know.

And you ain't near either, so why are you judging me?

And why does this pressure feel like a sudden urgency?

Mayday, I fear I've lost myself in all that I have seen.

I lost respect for some friends, I never thought they'd leave.

But I always come back each year so don't you worry.

Another year, another journal just full of stories.

I document it for the times that get real blurry.

For all the kids that were in too much of a hurry.

Insomnia.

I thought that if I wrote it out, I could let my mind flow.

The kids here are vultures, and this city never sleeps, but I'm searching for the high road.

I sit back and let them speak of some things that only I know.

For if I die before I wake, I'd hope that you'd hit me- I know.

Some things we'd never speak of, but trust me when I say,

Things were never meant to go only your way.

Yesterday, I lost my calculator.

I looked up to the stars for inspiration, but my perception somehow grew dimmer.

You see, there are no stars in sight, the world just didn't deliver.

I never learned direction, it was something I couldn't be messed with.

But I always found my way to the crowd, just a lonely little misfit.

I hate the light anyway. Why does it matter if the stars don't glow?

I hate the feeling of discomfort; do you mind if I don't show?

Because you see, I've been having problems.

But like the latest Texas Instrument, that was always required, I came equipped to solve them.

I seldom spoke up, I just couldn't be bothered,

But when I turned around, I regretted me harder.

Tampa Native.

In the bright of night, I think about why you hate me.

When the pain was over, I realized that it just ain't me.

My mama showed me strength, she told me to keep it going

My dad gave me faith, and lately, I think it's showing.

It's mind over matter I'm facing.

When I put the matter over mind, my heart gets to racing.

But when too many mind,

You're the last samurai;

And I don't think that I,

Can sit here and deny,

The laws that we have in motion; Inertia, it is a token.

No economy, but you get out what you put in.

They'll downgrade your worth until your blessing's now a lesson.

Good golly, I know you bee; But, them stings hurt.

Might have to start wearing a vest over my band shirts.

They never rest, aim for my chest until I bleed first;

But, my heart is on my sleeve so they leave hurt.

I guess it's me, I "couldn't be;" Yeah, that's what they say.

"She treats her people like she is putting them on layaway."

"She loves emotions, yeah she golden but she goes astray."

I go ghost at the first sight of broad day.

A Tampa native, no debating; yeah, that's who I am.

Got all these kids with their problems throwing stress on me.

They never cared, I was weird.

Now they check for me;

But I don't live on that street anymore,

I call it sesame.

Trust/ Sun.

It may sound odd, but I don't think I can trust the sun.

I know it takes on the burden of many, the pain has only begun.

No way one can be so cheery if the odds are close to none.

It may sound strange to ask, but who are you to the sun?

Intuition.

A ray of light divides the sky.

A beautiful sight to see, but it comes with a sigh.

You see, the light doesn't get to me.

It seems to passively shine over we,

And as it tries to stop she,

It will never down he.

A Poem By An Ex: Effort.

I can't be bothered

I can't be asked

In a few seconds, it won't matter

Nobody cares about the past

Uninterested in old treasures

Only in picking up new pleasures

Slaves to all-controlling vices

Like drinking, smoking, sex and rolling dices

No one can be bothered

No one can be asked

Too focused on getting cash to spend

Ignorant and self-serving until our ends.

R./A.

Revenge and acceptance go hand in hand

It controls the many and denies no man.

But, yet, it is not so simple to understand.

So, we add fear to what we "know" to get the upper hand.

For humans are so complex, it cannot be that simple;

When denial becomes acceptance, the revenge will drive you mental.

Intention.

Who is it that I'm missing?

More heartbreaks and separation to fuel my ambition.

I'm on a mission, to where? the destination is hidden.

I'm running around in circles just to erase what was written.

The given will remain given, you choose to pick my intention.

It's hard to smile in your face. After all, the past is what's written.

You give me nightmares at night. Still, I'm determined to fight.

Yes, I remember the call you where you'd "decided" to end your life.

Even after your operation and how glad we were when you made it.

Even when you lost your way, remember all the time that we wasted?

Laid back talking about life aligning plans.

I remembered again what it felt like to have a best friend.

In the darkest times of junior year, you were here;

But I had to let you go now you went and disappeared.

I don't know why it had to be this way, but I understand.

The stress is less so I won't question your intentions, man.

Summer Days.

As the summer days go slow, they start to grow longer.

My rest is cut short as my mind starts to wonder.

How could it be?

So pretty it starts at the beginning.

But we were both too scared to admit that we had a feeling.

My mind at ease with you, I don't know how you did it.

But I figure you're God's gift, my blessing;

So, yeah, let's get it.

I wanted to give you my best but somehow gave you my worst.

Now, I rip my heart off my sleeve so I can put it in a verse.

Got some things up off my chest so I know yours is heavier;

Finally opened up my heart and I couldn't think of a better carrier.

Lonely But Timeless.

Time never seems to end

You can never have too many "friends"

When the party's over, make amends.

For, time is not your only friend.

Silent Child.

In a world so big, I feel cold.

They tried to take advantage and it got old.

My soul grew cold, this I know.

When my mind gets dark, I go psycho.

But, insanity's a habit, and I deviate.

Writing more, I have to let the pain alleviate.

If I take it day by day, I'm destined to be golden.

A target by many, I've always been chosen.

Destined for despair, don't detest this golden child;

Karma starts at severe, the lucky get what's mild.

Hard to handle, I've always been a problem.

But unlike a child you know, I'm usually here to solve them.

Distractions will come in and take the focus if you let them,

My visions not so great but I can adjust to the stormy weather.

Now, admittedly, I don't know what you've been through;

But I'm here for the time being, just be glad that I chose you.

These words are my bond, I mean it, it's true.

Out of everybody out there, my connection is with you.

Don't let them steal, damage or break it.

Things like this take time, I promise you have to be patient.

God didn't build the world in one day; a pulse isn't formed
overnight,

But if you let the DNA form organically, I'm sure the
heartbeat will be just right.

I can't say what I don't know, so I choose to stay silent.

I heard silence was golden and I hope you don't mind it.

Loner Once More.

See how bright the stars shine at night?

We use the word bright but really, they're just dim.

Even the dark sky couldn't make them shine more than him.

I was a loner when you first found me, life was over.

So, I felt that much closer when you held me on your shoulder.

You must have had connections, there was no such thing as gravity

A bond formed between souls, couldn't stand when you were mad at me.

And if I could go back in time, the hands would stay in place.

It's hard to erase the many memories in your face.

Now a loner once more, I'll even the score;

Not looking for revenge I'm searching for something more.

Forevermore.

Dear anonymous,

I don't know how you'll spin the times they thought of us.

I don't know how you'll claim to be the victim, But I know that you blame me.

Might have them thinking that I'm crazy.

I know because I blamed me, had me thinking I was crazy.

To tell the truth, I just got lazy.

The kind words could no longer amaze me.

From the depths of my heart, with the blood pumping through my veins, I hoped that you could save me.

No, not you; I know this story sounds familiar.

To further complication, I'll paint a vaguer picture.

Proper plots take some time to develop; I learned life is all about how you do the setup.

So, I take proper measure to secure, that's the reason why I let up.

My path is golden, but I know even that depreciates in value.

It's an influx of people that take pleasure in the subsistence.

Behind closed doors wonder why they showed resistance.

I just have to ask, what's the reason you really hate me?

Is it because I was me when it went down and that's something you really wanted to be?

No, not me; but the you that you could be, and that's why you tried to gate me.

Your poor soul must have been confused so I'll let it be what it'll be;

And when two souls separate- the burden, I take with me.

I'm starting to think that I think too much,

But then I do believe that I don't think enough.

The times we shared are my memories,

I own them and no matter who you pretend to be,

I'll keep them near 'cause you're a friend of me

Forevermore, keep close my enemies.

Serendipity.

Everyone I held so dear, I watched them betray me;

All the ones I kept at bay looked at me crazy.

I couldn't see it then but they just wanted me;

But they don't know the pain that was in front of me.

I had to shield myself, it was-

Bad for my health, I don't-

Know what to say, but I-

Know that I'm safe, so now I-

Can sleep at night, I dream of-

A brighter life, I know that-

It'll be on time, I just have to-

Relieve my mind.

But, Mother?

How can I trust mother nature?

The concept is but a fraud.

I haven't seen, nor do I believe in your feeble God.

So cynical, but here I find comfort.

Under dark skies here, I get sunburnt.

But, mother, how can I trust nature?

All I see is evergreen, there must be more for me to see.

I can never remember father's time, so for the meanwhile, it's mine.

But, mother, how can I trust nature?

I'm tired of sitting around handing out favour's.

You told me I would grow but that's not verbatim.

If I had a choice, the green wouldn't show until later.

Oh, mother, I'll do you a favour;

I'll put my trust in mother nature.

The grass will grow, this I know.

The brighter days will surely show.

Oh, mother, you turned me into a lover.

I Want More!

The more confidence, the better.

Always keep your head up.

Leave before you get fed up;

But, never stay just to let up.

Your time is truly precious, don't let 'em just neglect you.

Stand up for what is better, never settle for what is lesser.

Remember all of your manners, because somebody taught you better.

I know it's hard to see the light, but you won't find it in the night.

Keep searching in the day, I'm sure you'll find your way.

We're all searching, don't you hide.

Never be ashamed and mask your pride.

Just let your Aura glow and be all you can be.

Turn over every rock, see all that you can see.

Akikya Q.

I'm writing this just for the stars, they don't shine as bright.

Put my soul into the sky, giving all my light.

Hopefully, it'll move the clouds away.

I love shapes, but right now I feel miles away.

They say never fear the moment dear,

For we were meant to light up the sky.

I could ask, but I don't wonder why.

As the seasons go by, I

Sit and watch the change.

Lord, I hate when it rains.

Subliminal messages of pain,

Silently screaming out your name.

Quiet head nods turn the other way,

What was more for there to say?

Our pride got in the way.

Remember sitting back thinking about what we would be someday.

You never knew, but me, I was always ready.

I learned early to reciprocate those who were steady.

My patience grew, but my mind got kind of heavy.

So now I write in the morning;

It's my conscience I'm trying to levy.

Oh, but it's three in the morning, am I losing my way?

Or maybe going back to the old me, I can't complain;

'Cuz when I wake in the morning it's all the same,

I got one more line for the doubts inside my brain,

The old forgot, but the new ones will remember my name.

-Akikya Q.

Vitae (Life).

A continuous path of unknown unknowns.

Just know it's okay to be alone.

Just know it's okay if you're not.

Any way you choose is fine, just never stay in the same spot.

Don't get too comfy on top, the fall is scary.

Don't feel so low at the bottom, nothing can be as merry.

Unlock every challenge and level up your rank.

Truly forgive yourself, even the devil was once a saint.

Love me for who I am, not who you assumed me to be. When we first met, my interest was slim; I love how you grew on me.

I told you you'd see me again. This page is for you; I love you!